THE LORD IS MY
SHEPHERD

JERRY BONSU

THE LORD IS MY SHEPHERD
I SHALL NOT WANT

With the creator of the universe as my
protector, provider and guide, I lack nothing.
Just like a shepherd who cares for his sheep,
God cares for me. And I am made complete.

John 10:11

*"I am the good shepherd. The good
shepherd gives his life for the sheep."*

HE MAKES ME TO LIE DOWN IN GREEN PASTURES

I'm blessed with a God who gives me strength
when I'm weak, rest when I'm tired,
and peace when I'm worried.

Matthew 11:28

*"Come to me, all of you who are tired
and have heavy loads. I will give you rest."*

HE LEADS ME BESIDE THE STILL WATERS

The good Shepherd leads me to a place where
worry can no longer reach me—So He can prosper me.
God makes my life abundant and my way secure.

John 4:14

*"...whoever drinks the water I give will never
be thirsty again. The water I give will become
a spring of water flowing inside him. It will
give him eternal life."*

HE RESTORES MY SOUL

God renew my strength, my mind, and my spirit each day. He removes my guilt and shame from messing up and gives me a fresh start in Jesus Christ.

2 Corinthians 5:17

"If anyone belongs to Christ, then he is made new.
The old things have gone; everything is made new."

HE LEADS ME TO THE PATH OF RIGHTEOUSNESS, FOR HIS NAME SEEK

For the good of His name, God leads me on paths that are right. Today, I'm grateful that the good Shepherd orders my steps in everything I do. To Him be all the glory, honor, and power forever.

Proverbs 3:3-4

"Don't ever stop being kind and truthful. Let kindness and truth show in all you do. Write them down in your mind as if on a tablet. Then you will be respected and pleasing to both God and men."

EVEN THOUGH I WALK THROUGH THE VALLEY OF THE SHADOW OF DEATH, I WILL FEAR NO EVIL, FOR YOU ARE WITH ME

Even when I walk through the dark scary, lonely places,
I won't be afraid because my Shepherd knows where I am.
He is here with me. He keeps me safe. He rescures me.
He makes me strong and brave. Dear Lord, I thank You
for always being by my side.

Hebrews 13:5[b]

*"I will never leave you;
I will never abandon you."*

YOUR ROD AND YOUR STAFF, THEY COMFORT ME

GOD

Your "**rod**" which is Your Word reminds me of Your authority, strength, power, Love, and Your protection. Your "**staff**" which is Your Spirit...**The Holy Spirit**, comfort me, guide me, lead me, teach me, counsel and strengthen me in every situation of life.

Isaiah 41:10[b]

*"...don't worry, because I am with you.
Don't be afraid, because I am your God."*

YOU PREPARE A TABLE BEFORE ME
IN THE PRESENCE OF MY ENEMIES

God, thank You for blessing me right in front of those
who don't like me. In their presence, You honor me.
You give me joy, peace, Love, and happiness.
I don't have to worry about what others say or think
about me, because I know that You has my back!

Deuteronomy 28:7

*"The Lord will let you defeat the enemies that
come to fight you. They will attack you from
one direction. But they will run from you in
seven directions."*

YOU ANOINT MY HEAD WITH OIL; MY CUP OVERFLOWS

Lord, Your blessings overwhelm me and I cannot count them all. My spirit is overwhelmed by the greatness of Your Love. Your anointing is with me, elevating me to the place You have called me to be... GREATNESS!

Genesis 12:2 (NIV)

"I will make you into a great nation, and I will bless you; I will make your name great, and you will be a blessing."

SURELY GOODNESS AND MERCY SHALL FOLLOW ME ALL THE DAYS OF MY LIFE

Like David, I'm convinced that God, who has taken such excellent care of me and my love once until now, will provide that same quality care for the rest of my life. As long as I live, goodness and mercy will be my portion in the mighty name of Jesus. AMEN!

Psalm 136:1

"Give thanks to the Lord because he is good.
His love continues forever."

AND I WILL DWELL IN THE HOUSE
OF THE LORD FOREVER

Oh God! My Shepherd, surely my life is safe in You.
Forever and ever, I will be in Your presence—where
I can find strength, comfort, peace and Love for my soul.
I will be Your child and You will be my father and
my friend...forever in Jesus name.
AMEN!

Psalm 84:10 [a]

*"One day in the courtyards of your (my) Temple
is better than a thousand days anywhere else."*

COLORING SESSION

THE LORD IS MY ....

I .... NOT ....

HE .... MY ....

YOU ANOINT .... WITH OIL ;

MY ....

SURELY .... AND .... SHALL

FOLLOW ME ....

....

I AM WHO GOD SAYS I AM

Biblical affirmations book for little boys & girls

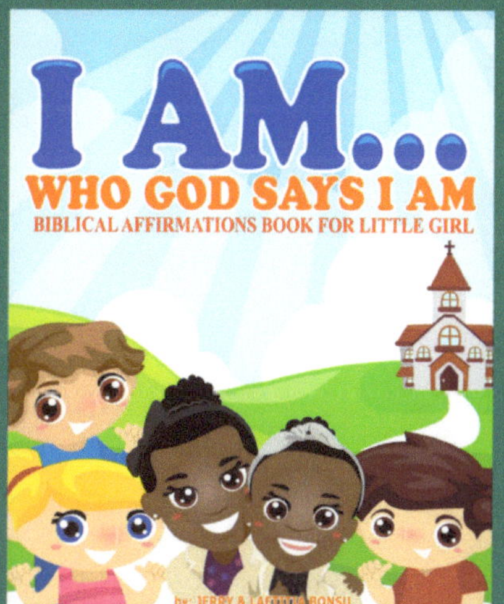

"*I believe that you can change your world by changing your words. Death and life are in the power of the tongue. That is why it is important to speak life and not death over your children... and help them to declare God's Word so that they can receive God's promises.*"

Jerry Bonsu

Biblical affirmations book for little girls

JERRY & LAETITIA BONSU

Biblical affirmations book for little boys

JERRY & LAETITIA BONSU

Available Now!!!

jerrybonsu.org